Days out in
Spring

Vic Parker

Heinemann
LIBRARY

Little Nippers

www.heinemann.co.uk/library
Visit our website to find out more information about **Heinemann Library** books.

To order:
☎ Phone 44 (0) 1865 888066
▤ Send a fax to 44 (0) 1865 314091
▱ Visit the Heinemann Bookshop at www.heinemann.co.uk/library to browse our
catalogue and order online.

First published in Great Britain by Heinemann
Library, Halley Court, Jordan Hill, Oxford
OX2 8EJ, part of Harcourt Education.
Heinemann is a registered trademark of Harcourt
Education Ltd.

Editorial: Jilly Attwood and Claire Throp
Design: Jo Hinton-Malivoire and bigtop,
Bicester, UK
Models made by: Jo Brooker
Picture Research: Rosie Garai, Sally Smith and
Debra Weatherley
Production: Séverine Ribierre

Originated by Dot Gradations
Printed and bound in China by South China
Printing Company

ISBN 0 431 17301 X (hardback)
08 07 06 05 04
10 9 8 7 6 5 4 3 2 1

ISBN 0 431 17306 0 (paperback)
08 07 06 05
10 9 8 7 6 5 4 3 2

British Library Cataloguing in Publication Data
Parker, Vic
Days out in spring
508.2
A full catalogue record for this book is available
from the British Library.

Acknowledgements
The publisher would like to thank the following
for permission to reproduce photographs:
Alamy p. **8–9** (Peter Usbeck); Angela Hampton
p. **14**; Ardea p. **7 top** (C. Jack & A. Bailey); Corbis
pp. **17**, **19**, **22** (Ariel Skelley), p. **16**; Cornish
Picture Library p. **20**; Gareth Boden p. **12–13**;
Getty Images pp. **11** (David Woodfall), **21**
bottom (Nicki Pardo), p. **4**; Imagestate p. **10**;
Martin Sookias p. **15**; Science Photo Library p. **21**
top (Claude Nuridsany & Marie Perennou); Steve
Behr/Stockfile pp. **6**, **18**, **23**; Trevor Clifford p. **5**;
Zefa p. **7 bottom** (M. Botek).

Cover photograph reproduced with permission of
Zefa/L. Buechner.

The publishers would like to thank Annie Davy
for her assistance in the preparation of this book.

Every effort has been made to contact copyright
holders of any material reproduced in this book.
Any omissions will be rectified in subsequent
printings if notice is given to the publishers.

The paper used to print this book comes from
sustainable resources.

Contents

It's springtime!

Trees and plants are growing.

4

Spring brings sunshine and showers.

What would you wear to go out?

5

Nature trail

What can you spot on a spring walk?

6

Look up high.
Birds nest among branches.

Look down low.
Ladybirds live among leaves.

7

At the stream

Take some bread for the ducks to nibble.

quack!

quack!

Watch them dabble and dive!

Farm babies

Lots of farm animals have babies in the spring.

pig

piglet

lamb

Hungry horses

Take some apples for the horse to **munch** and **crunch**.

Baby horses are called foals.

Buy a pet

Would you like an animal of your own?

In a pet shop, there are lots to choose from.

Do you know what rabbits like to eat?

Busy in the garden

Spring is a good time to
grow things in the garden.

Plant some seedlings in a row,
water them and watch
them grOW.

Teddy bears' picnic

It is fun to take
your teddy into
the garden for
a teatime treat.

Pond dipping

At the pond, creatures swim and crawl and hop everywhere.

20

Can you guess what this frogspawn will grow into?

21

Easter fun

What is this little girl hunting for?

Easter eggs!

Index

The end

Notes for adults

The *Days out in…* series helps young children become familiar with the way their environment changes through the year. The books explore the natural world in each season and how this affects community life and social activities. Used together, the books will enable discussion about similarities and differences between the seasons, how the natural world follows a cyclical pattern, and how different people mark special dates in the year. The following Early Learning Goals are relevant to this series:

Knowledge and understanding of the world
Early learning goals for exploration and investigation
• look closely at similarities, differences, patterns and change.
Early learning goals for sense of time
• observe changes in the environment, for example through the seasons.
Early learning goals for cultures and beliefs
• begin to know about their own cultures and beliefs and those of other people.

This book introduces the reader to the season of spring. It will encourage young children to think about spring weather, wildlife and landscape; activities they can enjoy in spring; and what clothes it is appropriate to wear. The book will help children extend their vocabulary, as they will hear new words such as *foal*, *seedling* and *frogspawn*. You may like to introduce and explain other new words yourself, such as *root* and *shoot*.

Additional information about the seasons
Not all places in the world have four seasons. Climate is affected by two factors: 1) how near a place is to the Equator (hence how much heat it receives from the Sun), 2) how high a place is (mountains are cooler than nearby lowlands). This is why some parts of the world have just two seasons, such as the hot wet season and the hot dry season across much of India. Other parts of the world have just one season, such as the year-long heat of the Sahara desert or the year-long cold of the North Pole.

Follow-up activities
• Draw a picture of a woodland scene in spring, with insects, animals, birds and people.
• Take a trip to a library to find out more about Easter and the spring festivals of other cultures.
• Dress up as spring animals and insects by making masks.